1/15

DISCARD

WRESTLING'S TOUGH GUYS

DOLPH ZIGGLER

by Matt Scheff

Consultant: Dr. Mike Lano
Pro Wrestling Writer, Photographer, and Radio Host

BEARPORT
PUBLISHING

New York, New York

Credits

Cover, © Sebastian Kahnert/dpa/Corbis; Title Page, © Sebastian Kahnert/dpa/picture-alliance/Newscom; TOC, © SI1 Wenn Photos/Newscom; 4L, © Sebastian Kahnert/dpa/picture-alliance/Newscom; 4R, © CD1 Wenn Photos/Newscom; 5, © SI1 Wenn Photos/Newscom; 6, © Rudy Balasko/Shutterstock; 7, © Duomo/Corbis; 8, © Zuma Press/Icon Sportswire; 9, © Ken Love/MCT/Newscom; 10, © Ed Webster; 11, © s_bukley/Shutterstock; 12, © Mike Lano Photography; 13, © Mike Lano Photography; 14, © Zuma Press/Alamy; 15, © SI1 Wenn Photos/Newscom; 16, © DPA/ABACA/Newscom; 17, © Mike Lano Photography; 18, © Zuma Press/Alamy; 19, © SI1 Wenn Photos/Newscom; 20, © Moses Robinson/Getty Images; 21, © Shamsuddin Muhammad; 22T, © SI1 Wenn Photos/Newscom; 22B, © SI1 Wenn Photos/Newscom.

Publisher: Kenn Goin
Editor: Natalie Lunis
Creative Director: Spencer Brinker
Photo Researcher: Chrös McDougall
Design: Debrah Kaiser

Library of Congress Cataloging-in-Publication Data in process at time of publication (2015)
Library of Congress Control Number: 2014041537
ISBN-13: 978-1-62724-549-4

For more information, write to Bearport Publishing Company, Inc., 45 West 21st Street, Suite 3B, New York, New York 10010. Printed in the United States of America.

10 9 8 7 6 5 4 3 2 1

Contents

Claiming the Belt

Boos filled the arena as Dolph Ziggler stepped into the ring. It was August 2010, and Dolph was one of the biggest **heels** in the **WWE**. On this night, he was battling the popular Kofi Kingston for the **Intercontinental Championship**.

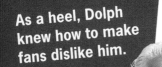
As a heel, Dolph knew how to make fans dislike him.

Kofi Kingston

Dolph took control of the match early. Then the tables turned as Kofi nailed him with a high-flying kick called Trouble in Paradise. Dolph was down. It looked like this was it for him! Then, before anyone knew what was happening, he pulled himself to his feet. Dolph leaped into the air, grabbed Kofi by the head, and slammed him to the mat in a move Dolph calls the **Zig-Zag**. The referee counted 1-2-3. It was over! Dolph was the new champion!

Dolph shows off one of his championship belts.

The Intercontinental Championship was Dolph's first major WWE singles belt.

5

A Kid with a Dream

Before Dolph was a wrestling champion, he was a big-time wrestling fan. He was born in Cleveland, Ohio, on July 27, 1980, and given his real name—Nicholas Theodore Nemeth. Growing up, Nicholas loved to watch boxing and **mixed martial arts**. His favorite sport, however, was wrestling. He went to his first WWE match at age five. From that moment on, he was hooked.

Cleveland is the second biggest city in Ohio.

Before he reached his early teens, Nicholas joined a youth wrestling program. He was disappointed, however, after his first practice. "I walked in and went, 'Where are the ropes and the **turnbuckles**?'" he remembers. Nicholas quickly learned that **amateur** wrestlers battle on mats and focus on **grappling**. He would have to wait to get into the ring and perform huge moves like his WWE heroes.

Hulk Hogan was one of wrestling's biggest stars while Nicholas was growing up.

Nicholas's wrestling heroes included Hulk Hogan, Ric Flair, and Shawn Michaels.

Amateur Star

Although Nicholas felt let down, he decided to stick with amateur wrestling. His sturdy, athletic build made him a natural for the sport. Once he started high school and joined the wrestling team, Nicholas became a star. His victories on the mat helped his team win two national championships.

Amateur wrestling is an Olympic sport. Many U.S. high schools have teams.

Nicholas tallied 82 pins as a student at St. Edward High School in Ohio. As a result, he holds the school record.

After high school, Nicholas put his dream of being a pro wrestler on hold so he could attend Kent State University in Ohio. He studied **political science** there and also earned a spot on Kent State's wrestling team. As a college athlete, he continued to stand out. He went on to win three Mid-America Conference (MAC) championships in the 165-pound (75 kg) class.

Kent State University

Going Pro

After graduating from college in 2003, Nicholas was ready to start training to become a pro wrestler. He also had a backup plan, however. In case wrestling didn't work out, he would become a lawyer. He was even accepted into law school. Before the school year started, though, Nicholas got a surprise. The WWE invited him to a tryout!

Nicholas weighed just 165 pounds (75 kg) when he had his first WWE tryout. Today, he weighs 215 pounds (97.5 kg).

In his first tryout for the WWE, Nicholas took on a wrestler who outweighed him by 100 pounds (45 kg)! The match helped him understand that he needed to be bigger and stronger to make it in the WWE.

The WWE **scouts** who watched the tryout thought Nicholas had **potential**. They suggested that he should bulk up and try again later. After that, Nicholas put all of his effort into wrestling. Once he reached a strapping 221 pounds (100 kg), he tried out again. This time the scouts signed him. He was officially a pro wrestler!

Nicholas has said he still might go to law school once he is done wrestling.

A Taste of the Big Time

Nicholas began wrestling at Ohio Valley Wrestling, a training league where new WWE wrestlers could work on their skills. Because he was quick and powerful, he quickly developed into a successful wrestler. Then, in September 2005, he got good news. He was being brought up to wrestle in the WWE!

Before wrestling in the WWE, Nicholas trained at Ohio Valley Wrestling.

Becoming a WWE star was another story, though. After his first few matches, it was clear that fans weren't warming up to him. So Nicholas took time off to develop a new character. A few months later, he returned—this time playing the **role** of a male cheerleader named Nicky in a group called the Spirit Squad. By November 2006, however, fans had rejected that character, too. Nicholas would have to try again.

Nicholas (right) and members of the Spirit Squad show off their tag team belts.

The Spirit Squad wasn't a total failure for Nicholas. He won the **tag team** belt during that time. It was his first WWE championship.

A New Character

After two unsuccessful runs in the WWE, Nicholas struggled as a pro wrestler. For almost two more years, he went back to a training league, wrestling in front of smaller crowds. He used several **ring names** during this time, including Nic Nemeth and The Natural.

Nicholas (top) throws another wrestler out of the ring during a 2008 Florida Championship Wrestling match.

Nicholas finally returned to the WWE in September 2008. When he came back, he had created a new character and a new name—Dolph Ziggler. Dolph was a heel who made fans mad with his constant cheating. He became even more of a bad guy when he started a **feud** with fan favorite Kofi Kingston. The feud peaked in 2010 when Dolph beat Kofi three matches in a row and earned the WWE Intercontinental Championship.

Dolph's character was known for being very confident. Fans sometimes booed him for being too confident.

As Dolph Ziggler, Nicholas bleached his hair so it was bright blond. The new look fit Dolph's loud and brash personality.

The Rise of Ziggler

After 2008, Dolph's struggles to make it were over. Fans loved both his high-flying wrestling skills and his attention-grabbing **antics**. They even started calling him The Showoff.

Dolph (right) battles actor Hugh Jackman in a 2011 show.

The Zig-Zag is one of Dolph's **signature moves**. The Blond Ambition is another. To perform this move, Dolph faces his opponent and then jumps onto his back, driving his opponent's face into the mat.

By 2011, Dolph was one of the WWE's biggest stars. In one show in February of that year, he was even awarded the World Heavyweight Championship belt. However, he lost it to Edge only 11 minutes later! A few months after that, Dolph won his third championship when he beat his old **foe** Kofi Kingston. Dolph put Kofi in a sleeper hold. Kofi couldn't breathe! The match had to be stopped, and Dolph took the United States championship. He held this belt for six months!

Dolph (left) battles Zack Ryder in a 2012 match.

Climbing to the Top

The next goal for Dolph was winning back the World Heavyweight Championship. In July 2012, he got an amazing opportunity. Dolph was one of eight wrestlers chosen for a Money in the Bank match. To win, somebody had to climb a ladder and grab a briefcase hanging above the ring. Whoever won the briefcase could challenge for any WWE belt at any time. Dolph grabbed the briefcase first to win the challenge!

Dolph climbs into the ring.

In 2011, reporters who write about pro wrestling named Dolph the Most Improved Wrestler of the year.

Dolph waited until the perfect time to challenge another wrestler for the World Heavyweight **title**. Finally, in April 2013, he saw that champion Alberto Del Rio was hurting. So Dolph challenged Alberto and easily won back the World Heavyweight title. This time he held it for about two months.

Alberto Del Rio

Bright Future

Dolph Ziggler's wrestling career didn't take off right away. Once he showed up as a great character, however, he quickly became a star. Dolph started out as a heel, but he has also been a **babyface** at times. Either way, he has shown off his powerful moves, from the Zig-Zag to the high-flying Blond Ambition.

Dolph prepares to hit Zack Ryder with a move called a neck breaker.

Dolph won his fifth individual title belt in the summer of 2014. He beat The Miz to win the Intercontinental Championship.

Dolph is also one of a handful of WWE superstars who has enjoyed success both as an amateur and a professional wrestler. What does the future hold for him? Will he be a heel or a babyface? For many fans, it doesn't matter. They know he'll be a force in the WWE for years to come.

Dolph is one of the WWE's biggest stars.

The Dolph Ziggler File

Stats:

Real name:	Nicholas "Nick" Theodore Nemeth
Born:	July 27, 1980
Height:	6'0" (1.8 m)
Weight:	215 pounds (97.5 kg)
Greatest moves:	Zig-Zag, Blond Ambition

Fun Facts:

- Nicholas is able to communicate in American Sign Language.

- Nicholas chose the name Dolph because it was his grandfather's name. A friend suggested the last name Ziggler, and it stuck.

- One of Dolph's nicknames is The Showoff because he loves to show off his skills and his muscles in the ring.

Glossary

amateur (AM-uh-chur) an athlete, such as a high school or college player, who is not paid to compete

antics (AN-tiks) funny or wild actions

babyface (BAY-bee-*fayss*) a wrestler whom most fans view as a hero or a good guy

feud (FYOOD) an intense competition between two or more wrestlers that can last for weeks or months

foe (FOH) an enemy

grappling (GRAP-uhl-ing) a type of fighting where wrestlers tangle with each other while staying close together

heels (HEELZ) wrestlers whom fans view as villains or bad guys

Intercontinental Championship (*in*-tur-*kon*-tuh-NEN-tuhl CHAM-pee-uhn-*ship*) one of the WWE's wrestling titles; a wrestler often competes for this title before wrestling for one of the WWE's bigger titles

mixed martial arts (MIKST MAR-shuhl ARTS) a sport that includes a variety of fighting styles, including moves from wrestling and boxing

political science (puh-LIT-uh-kuhl SYE-uhnss) the study of government and politics

potential (puh-TEN-shuhl) the ability to achieve something

ring names (RING NAYMZ) the names that wrestlers use while in the ring; usually not the wrestlers' real names

role (ROHL) an acting part

scouts (SKOUTS) people who have the job of finding talented athletes for a team, group, or league

signature moves (SIG-nuh-chur MOOVZ) special moves that a wrestler becomes known for using

tag team (TAG TEEM) a wrestling event in which two-person teams battle each other; usually only one wrestler from each team is allowed in the ring at a time and teammates switch places inside and outside the ring by "tagging," or hand-slapping, each other

title (TYE-tuhl) a championship

turnbuckles (TURN-buhk-uhlz) devices that connect the ropes in each corner of a wrestling ring

WWE (DUHB-*uhl*-yoo DUHB-*uhl*-yoo EE) World Wrestling Entertainment, the leading pro wrestling organization in the world

Zig-Zag (ZIG-zag) one of Dolph's finishing moves; he jumps high into the air, grabs his opponent from behind, and then slams the opponent's back onto the ground

Bibliography

Burke, David. "WWE Star Ziggler is Living His Dream," Go&Do (August 30, 2012).

DolphZiggler.com

Herron, Gary. "WWE's Dolph Ziggler Once Planned on Law Career," *Rio Rancho Observer* (May 26, 2010).

Wells, Kevin. "Interview: Dolph Ziggler, Former WWE Heavyweight Champion," Communities Digital News (January 28, 2014).

Read More

Gordon, Nick. *Dolph Ziggler*. Minneapolis, MN: Bellwether (2012).

Scheff, Matt. *Kofi Kingston*. Minneapolis, MN: ABDO (2014).

St. John, Chris. *Wrestling*. New York: PowerKids Press (2012).

Learn More Online

To learn more about Dolph Ziggler, visit
www.bearportpublishing.com/WrestlingsToughGuys

Index